COUNTING
WITH
COMMON CENTS
Nick's Tricks

Written By:
Deirdre McCarthy

Illustrated By:
Angela Rizza

ISBN: 1541017560
ISBN 13: 9781541017566
Library of Congress Control Number: 2015906958
CreateSpace Independent Publishing Platform
North Charleston, South Carolina

Dedicated to: Garrett and John Atticus

I am standing next to the tree.

Do you see me waving?
I want to show you tricks about
counting and saving.

Hi! My name is Nickel, but you can call me Nick.
When it comes to counting, I am pretty quick.

I am worth 5 cents you see...
To count faster, count by me.

You can count fast too,
if you try.
Let's get started.
Don't be shy!

As we go, here are the tricks
you should know:

When you count... Here is the key...
5 pennies are always the same as me!

When you save... You should know...
The amount will always grow.

Now...
Let's try counting and saving
around the money tree!

But...
To begin, we must first
arrive at the number...

FIVE: 5
WOW! You are so smart.
I can see we are off to a GREAT start.
Let's follow the wren.
She will take us to the number...

TEN: 10

Ten pennies, two nickels, or a dime...
Looks like it's counting and saving time.
Let's find the Ant Queen. She will lead us to the number...

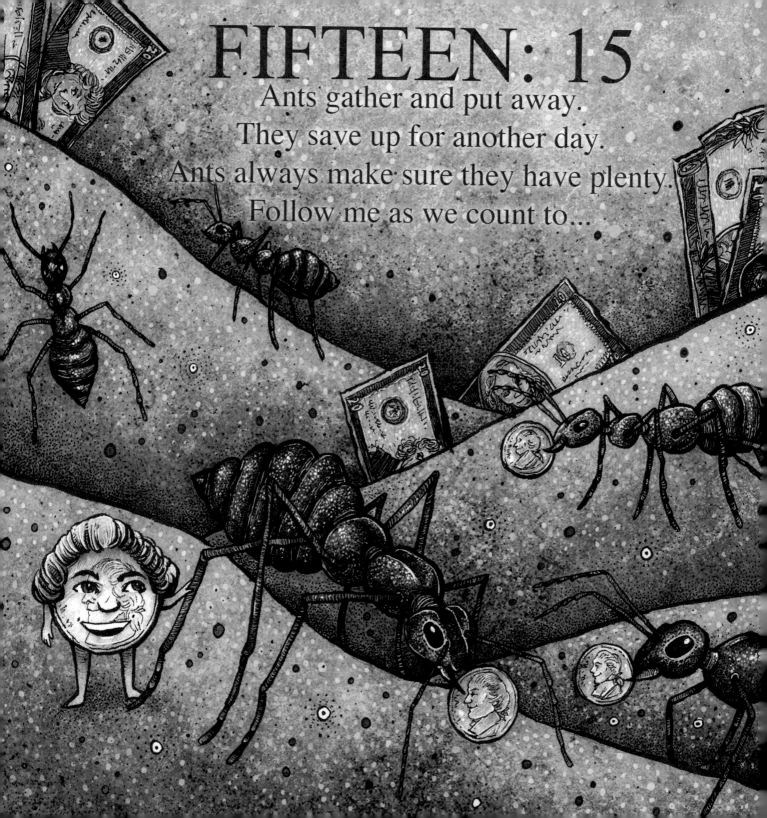

FIFTEEN: 15

Ants gather and put away.
They save up for another day.
Ants always make sure they have plenty.
Follow me as we count to...

TWENTY: 20

Sweet honey is what bees love to store.
They always work to make and save more.

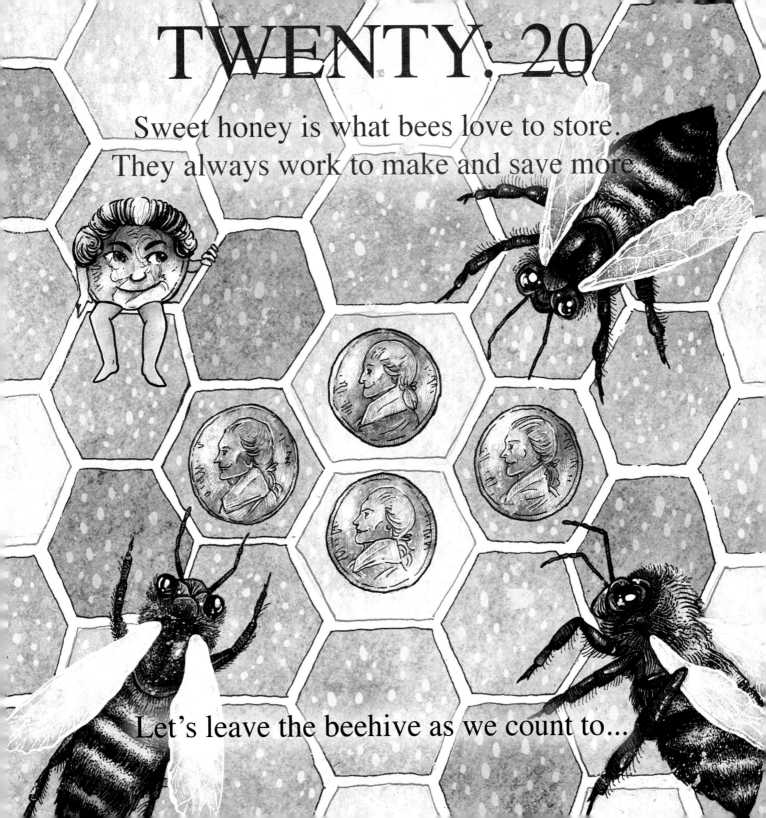

Let's leave the beehive as we count to...

TWENTY FIVE: 25

Beavers work to save logs and sticks.
They love my counting and saving tricks.
That dam is sturdy so let's move on to the number...

THIRTY: 30

See the birds doing their best.
They work hard to build a nest.
Watch the eggs come alive as we count to..

THIRTY FIVE: 35

Look at the chipmunks run and scurry.
Counting and saving makes them hurry.
These chipmunks are so sporty.
They will take us to number...

FORTY: 40

The sly fox saves in places no one can see.
He makes sure there is enough for his family.
When it comes to saving, the fox will thrive.

Now, let's count to...

FORTY FIVE: 45

When it comes to spending, turtles go slow.
They like to see the coin amount grow.
My counting and saving tricks are really nifty.

Let's move on to the number...

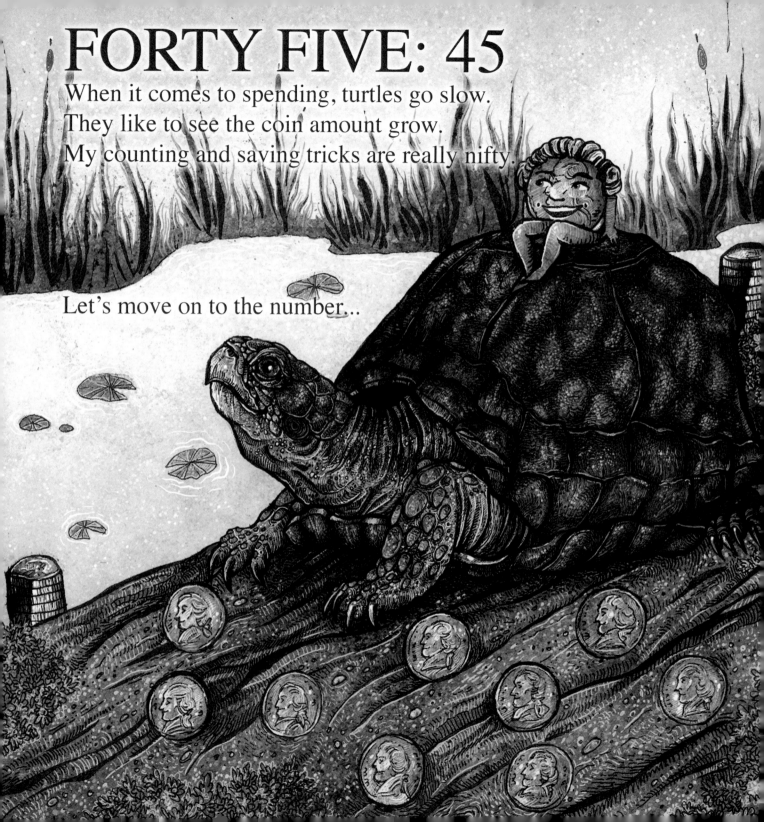

FIFTY: 50

Fifty cents...
The owl is so wise.
He will save this counting prize.

That was a BLAST!
You are on your way
to counting fast.

You are now my counting friend!
Follow me to reach...
THE...

END!

REMEMBER my tricks.
When you count...
Here is the key...
5 pennies are always the same as me.

When you save...
You should know...
The amount will always grow.

NICK!

FUN FACTS

1. The first "Nickel" was minted in 1866, right after the American Civil War.

2. The Shield Nickel was made out of 75% copper and 25% nickel.

3. The Liberty Head or V Nickel was minted from 1883 to 1913.

4. The reverse of the coin depicted the Roman Numeral V for 5, to denote the denomination.

5. 1913 Liberty Head Nickels are extremely rare. In 2010, one went for $3,737,500 at auction.

6. The Buffalo or Indian Head Nickel was minted from 1913 to 1938.

7. The Jefferson Nickel has been minted from 1938 to present.

8. The front of the coin pictures a profile of Thomas Jefferson, the third President of the United States.

9. The reverse of the coin pictures, Monticello, Jefferson's house.

10. The back reads: "E PLURIBUS UNUM", which means, "ONE FROM MANY".

Made in the USA
Lexington, KY
14 December 2018